D0830395

Thirty Days of
Thanksgiving

Sue Boldt

Thirty Days of

Thanksgiving

All scripture quotations, unless otherwise indicated, are taken from the New King James Version®. Copyright © 1982 by Thomas Nelson, Inc. Used by permission. All rights reserved.

Scripture quotations marked (NLT) are taken from the Holy Bible, New Living Translation, copyright ©1996, 2004, 2015 by Tyndale House Foundation. Used by permission of Tyndale House Publishers, Inc., Carol Stream, Illinois 60188. All rights reserved.

Scripture quotations taken from the Amplified® Bible (AMPC), Copyright © 1954, 1958, 1962, 1964, 1965, 1987 by The Lockman Foundation Used by permission. www.lockman.org

Scripture quotations marked MSG are taken from *THE MESSAGE*, copyright © 1993, 2002, 2018 by Eugene H. Peterson. Used by permission of NavPress. All rights reserved. Represented by Tyndale House Publishers, Inc.

Cover Photo: Nathan Dumlao, *Unsplash*

Thirty Days of

Dedication

To the seven reasons I am deliriously grateful to God for:

Avriella
Nolan
Finley
Weston
Remy
Lucy
Penelope

Thirty Days of

Introduction

I would like to think that I have been a Jesus follower and worshiper of Him for some time, now. Nevertheless, for years, I would often allow the busyness of life, family, work, ministry – you name it – to confine my thanksgiving, praise, and worship to the hour and a half when I joined my church family at a weekend service with an awesome worship band leading the way. And of course, I most definitely had times alone of great thankfulness to Him for the wondrous things He had done in my life. Nothing wrong with that, nevertheless, there was ever so much more.

Some years ago, with the Holy Spirit's prompting, I made a decision to live in Jesus' presence no matter what.

There is an indiscernibly fine line between the Spirit's call and our simple *yes*. What He does and what we do is often blurred, but our *yes* is important. I think Jesus simply said, "Baby-girl, you have wasted enough time, I have so much more I want to do in and through you." That is when I decided that as much as was in me – this piece of often wayward dust, infilled with the Holy Spirit – I would move heaven, earth, and even hell, to be filled with a sense of God's presence every day of my life that I drew breath. I had read in God's Word this manner of life in the Spirit was possible and available and I had become hungry enough to want to pursue it – to pursue Him. What I found was tremendous healing, love, deliverance, grace, peace, and joy. What gifts!

Certainly, I have not lived up to this hope and decision as perfectly as I would like. I am a work in progress. Nevertheless, my simple *yes* transformed my life in ways I could never conceive – even after thirty-five years in pastoral ministry. One of the most notable distinctions that I encountered was the fresh and spontaneous gratitude, praise, and worship that began to flow from my heart and lips in my home, workplace, and marketplace.

What you hold in your hands is an enhanced version of an online Bible Study I recently led. You will find the readings are short and easy. After each devotional, you will be encouraged to ponder and expand your own gratefulness and worship to the Lord. These interactive pages *are* somewhat different from one another. Please read them carefully and respond as your heart is leading you.

I pray this little volume regarding gratitude, praise, and worship will be a blessing for you through a month of days – any month by the way, not just November. And that you will receive, at the least, a small portion of the blessing I had in writing it. And living it.

Are you ready? I am! Let's enjoy our King and exalt His Name together for the next thirty days, and the next thirty days, and the next thirty – forever . . .

In HIM,
Sue

Thanksgiving

Day 1

I beseech you therefore, brethren, by the mercies of God,
that you present your bodies a living sacrifice, holy,
acceptable to God, which is your reasonable service.
Romans 12:1

As we embark upon this journey of thanksgiving, praise, and worship through God's Word, let's begin at the beginning.

Surrender.

Yes, surrender is the ultimate act of worship and gratefulness.

And surrender is where we find our true selves – who we were meant to be from the hand Who so lovingly created us. Really. When we lose ourselves to Him, we find life at its fullest, most satisfying, and most complete.

So, you see, we can sing all the songs, raise our hands, and shout praise all we want but real rubber meets the road when we allow the Holy Spirit to pour out our small, selfish, limited lives for HIS large, love beyond reason, priceless, and boundless adventure for us. Because surrender means we trust Him, and when we trust Jesus, we worship with all our being.

From Genesis to Revelation, we discover that the Almighty, Who flung the galaxies into existence like glitter from His hand, ever and only wants – our hearts. He desires us to desire Him and there is no greater act of love and honor we can bestow our heavenly Father than the gift of ourselves.

So, let's do this thing. This thing that so often trips us up, is so much easier said than done at first, and requires every ounce of our being. Let's offer our lives to the One Who holds every detail that concerns us in the tenderness of His heart. Let's surrender everything to Jesus. Let's worship Him by giving Him our all.

Ten things I am surrendering to Him as I worship . . .

- _____
- _____
- _____
- _____
- _____
- _____
- _____
- _____
- _____
- _____

How does today's devotional speak to me personally?

_____
_____
_____
_____
_____

He who finds his life will lose it,
and he who loses his life for My sake will find it.
Matthew 10:39

This verse in my own words . . .

_____
_____
_____
_____

Day 2

Let everything that has breath praise the Lord!
Psalm 150:6

It doesn't get much simpler than this!

This last verse of the last of the Psalms declares that if you and are breathing, we had better get our praise on. I am pretty sure no one is exempt.

If you and I are alive at this moment – which I am assuming we are – then Lord Jesus is worthy of all our worship and praise. Think of it – it is His breath that gave us life in the first place (Genesis 2:7). And in return, we discover that our life's oxygen is to worship Him with that very breath!

The tender act in the Garden of Eden – where it all began for humanity – was God sharing with us His very own breath of life. And now, those who have received Christ by faith (John 1:12) have also been filled with the life-breath power of the Holy Spirit (John 20:22). Indeed. The original Hebrew and Greek words defined *Spirit* in our English mean *breath, to breathe, breeze, and wind.*

The early church apologist, Ireneaus of Lyons, penned, *the glory of God is man fully alive.* We *are* fully alive when we worship as we intentionally press into the throne room of the Holy of Holies and allow the Holy Spirit to catch us up with the heavenly hosts.

So, it is time to praise. Time to direct our adoration upward. Time to remember He holds our breath in His hands and owns all our ways (Daniel 5:23b). It is time to inhale a deep breath of the Holy Spirit and exhale with new words and phrases that describe our King.

It is time for us to revel in His love and not hold back. It is time for everything and everyone that has breath to praise Him.

Ten things I worship Him for in this moment...

- _____
- _____
- _____
- _____
- _____
- _____
- _____
- _____
- _____
- _____

How does today's devotional speak to me personally?

_____

_____

_____

_____

_____

Now to the King eternal, immortal, invisible, to God who alone is wise, be honor and glory forever and ever. Amen.
1 Timothy 1:17

My own words of worship...

_____

_____

_____

_____

Day 3

Let the high praises of God be in their mouth,
And a two-edged sword in their hand,
Psalm 149:6

Let's be reminded, worship is often warfare.

When we worship, breakthrough takes place in the heavenly realm that can miraculously change circumstances in our physical realm. Yes, worship can do this. There are just too many Bible stories that record this and too many life experiences to discount it.

Our enemy, the devil, and his demons can't stand it when we worship. It is genuinely the worst sound in their ears. Our praise sends them running. Psalm 149 further tells us that the demonic are bound up. In addition, when we get our eyes off our circumstances and turn them to the One Who is Almighty and reigns supreme, our situations appear minuscule in His hand. Worship aligns our hearts with His heart to hear His battle commands for us. Worship humbles us to know that only He can fight on our behalf. And, worship positions us to win the battle of whatever we are facing.

Instead of getting angry, worship.
Instead of allowing anxiety to rule, praise.
Instead of succumbing to self-pity, lift up the One Who uplifts you.

No, we don't worship to get. Nevertheless, when we do genuinely worship the King of Kings and Lord of Lords, fears cease, the enemy falters, Jesus is glorified, and His presence transforms us.

So, whatever you are facing right now, instead of contacting someone else, first go to the throne room. Remember who God is and lift your praise. Stay until you have touched heaven. Ask for a scripture to strengthen you, then see what He does next. Because truly – worship is warfare.

Ten worship statements to speak to the King of Heaven's Armies . . .

- _____
- _____
- _____
- _____
- _____
- _____
- _____
- _____
- _____
- _____

How does today's devotional speak to me personally?

_____
_____
_____
_____

... he appointed those who should sing to the LORD, and who should praise the beauty of holiness, as they went out before the army and were saying: "Praise the LORD, For His mercy endures forever."
2 Chronicles 20:21

A declaration of God's greatness over a difficult circumstance I am facing.

_____
_____
_____
_____

Day 4

...To give thanks to Your holy name,
To triumph in Your praise.
Psalms 106:47b

In the selflessness of the Trinity – the Father, the Son, and the Holy Spirit - our praise and gratitude not only bring Him glory but also cause us to be participants in His *triumph*.

Our God is not egocentric, self-absorbed, or self-centered. Honestly. He doesn't need us. He doesn't need our worship. *We need* our worship of Him. Worship positions us to see God's face. And as we glimpsed yesterday, the enemy needs to hear us worship our Abba Father.

Many years ago, when I was a young girl, my dad would attempt to teach me to dance. The old-fashioned, ever so elegant dance where I placed my hand on his shoulder that I could barely reach. And with his arm around my young waist, stooping down to reach me, he led me through graceful steps. However, if I looked down at my feet, I would stumble, but when I looked up into his face and trusted his leading and guiding me – oh, what sweet moments. Our walk with the Lord is so much like this dance. Our worship is our looking directly upon His face.

Have you ever walked into a pitch-black, darkened room? You simply need to hit the switch. LIGHT! Darkness flees. That pretty much sums up what happens when we worship and praise. Triumph takes place. We sense the Holy Spirit causing faith to rise in our hearts. Yes, worship is *for us*. No wonder we find Paul and Silas worshipping when facing down death. (Acts 16:25).

Find a place today where you can be *alone* with Him. Tell the Lord how much you love Him. You will be hard-pressed to tell me that something did not happen for you: a little bit of triumph and a whole lot of darkness fleeing.

Ten worship phrases about God's character (i.e. love, kindness, goodness)...

- _____
- _____
- _____
- _____
- _____
- _____
- _____
- _____
- _____
- _____

How does today's devotional speak to me personally?

_____

_____

_____

_____

But at midnight Paul and Silas were praying and singing hymns to God,
. . .Suddenly there was a great earthquake . . .
and immediately all the doors were opened
and everyone's chains were loosed.
Acts 16:25-26

What cares in my life could I choose to worship instead of worrying?

_____

_____

_____

Day 5

So Jesus answered and said,
"Were there not ten cleansed? But where are the nine?
Were there not any found who returned
to give glory to God except this foreigner?"
And He said to him, "Arise, go your way.
Your faith has made you well."
Luke 17:17-19

We can't ponder thanksgiving and worship without talking about the ten lepers. Only *ONE* came back to thank Lord Jesus?? Yet how often have I been guilty of the very same thing?

As we surrender our lives in greater measure to the Lord Jesus, we will find that our gratefulness will become more and more evident. A surrendered life means trusting Him fully with how He will handle the small and large concerns that we face. When we give up control to Him, we begin to recognize that God does know what He is doing. We then get out of the way to let Him reveal His love in ways we didn't realize before. Gratefulness will become a *spontaneous* fountain from our hearts and lips. Trust me. I know this from my own life.

Think of gratefulness to Him as the temperature gauge of *who* is in control: is it me or my Heavenly Father? Ponder that for a bit…

Intentional gratefulness is the greatest cure for discouragement. It beats out the blues. It drowns out the voice of self-pity, and it can be a tool to overcome depression and anxiety. Indeed, there are many factors regarding these instances, but from personal experience and years of offering pastoral counseling, I am hard-pressed to find people who live daily in effervescent gratefulness who are down for the count for very long.

When the thankful, now-healed leper returned to Jesus, he must have immensely blessed the Lord's heart. Let's be people who bless our Redeemer's heart, too.

Ten things I am grateful for today . . .

- _____
- _____
- _____
- _____
- _____
- _____
- _____
- _____
- _____
- _____

How does today's devotional speak to me personally?

_____
_____
_____
_____
_____

That I may proclaim with the voice of thanksgiving,
And tell of all Your wondrous works.
Psalm 26:7

A short prayer of gratitude for His wondrous works in my life . . .

_____
_____
_____
_____

Day 6

...saying with a loud voice: "Worthy is the Lamb who was slain
To receive power and riches and wisdom,
And strength and honor and glory and blessing!"
Revelation 5:12

Praise and worship can open our spiritual eyes to recognize and experience our position with Christ in heavenly places (Ephesians 2:6). As denominational president and pastor, Randy Remington, states, *worship interrupts our preoccupation with ourselves.*[1] And when we truly enter His presence with our thanksgiving and praise, it opens our spirit to the Biblical truth that we are already hidden in Him and reigning with Him.

Genuine worship causes our faith to rise. Honest worship gets our gaze off our stuff and onto Who He is and who we are in Him. Holy Spirit inspired worship positions us to receive from our Father what He lavishly desires to bestow upon us. When we join the chorus of the heavenly hosts worshipping around God's throne, our true home – heaven – starts to rub off on us.

It can be so formidable for us who have schedules to keep, dishes to wash, kiddos to chase after, and cars to fix to remember that we are already living in the Kingdom of His love (Colossians 1:13). In our daily stuff, it can be so challenging to remember that we are seated with Him above principalities and powers – the devil and his minions – who would attempt to destroy our lives (John 10:10a). And amid all that assails us, it can be difficult to remember that we are more than conquerors through Him who loves us (Romans 8:37).

Yet, we don't worship to get. We worship because He is Worthy. Nevertheless, worship reminds us of our actual position in Christ. His cross purchased our entrance into heavenly realms even while our feet are planted here on earth.

What a sublime gift worship is.

Ten characteristics of God I love . . .

- _____
- _____
- _____
- _____
- _____
- _____
- _____
- _____
- _____
- _____

How does today's devotional speak to me personally?

_____
_____
_____
_____

All the angels stood around the throne . . .saying:
Amen! Blessing and glory and wisdom,
Thanksgiving and honor and power and might,
Be to our God forever and ever. Amen.
Revelation 7:11-12

I will take a moment to worship Him now. What emotions fill my heart?

_____
_____
_____

Day 7

... but be filled with the Spirit,
speaking to one another in psalms and hymns and spiritual songs, singing
and making melody in your heart to the Lord,
giving thanks always for all things to God the Father
in the name of our Lord Jesus Christ,
Ephesians 5:18-20

I have a question for you. Hasn't music played a large part in your life?

Music is powerful. God created us to be moved by the tapestry of its various sounds, beats, and beauty. It only takes a familiar song from a certain time in your life to draw you back into memories, emotions, and recollections. We can usually long remember the lyrics to a song. A memorized piece of literature? Maybe not so much.

We find music integral in thanksgiving and praise in the halls of heaven and throughout the ages on earth (Revelation 5:12). Often the Holy Spirit speaks to us through melodies and lyrics to build our faith and usher us into the throne room. Spirit-filled worship music is transformative, changing us, and the atmosphere around us (Psalm 22:3).

Years ago, our family struggled to get back to God's will for our lives after we had taken a drastic detour. We needed to return to where we had last heard His direction, and it required every ounce of our faith and trust. That season for us felt as if we were jumping off a cliff into His unknown.

During that time, my husband and I arrived to worship with our church every time the doors were opened. We went to four services every weekend, just to partake of the authentic, Spirit-led worship there. As we entered into God's presence, the Holy Spirit anointed songs of worship and praise caused our fears to dissipate, fresh surrender took place, and our faith was released.

And, God came through for us.

My favorite worship songs that usher me into His presence . . .

- _____
- _____
- _____
- _____
- _____
- _____
- _____
- _____
- _____
- _____

How does today's devotional speak to me personally?

_____

_____

_____

_____

_____

Serve the LORD with gladness;
Come before His presence with singing.
Psalm 100:2

My own words of worship . . .

_____

_____

_____

_____

Day 8

God is Spirit,
and those who worship Him must worship in spirit and truth.
John 4:24

Lord Jesus speaks these words to the woman at the well. She knows she has just encountered Eternity, and now she is questioning Him about the proper method, place, and propriety of offering our adoration. Jesus cuts to the chase. It doesn't really matter how, when, or where we worship but that when we do, it is Holy Spirit ignited and filled with truth. How is this done? Today, let's look at worshiping in spirit.

Our *spirit* is the unseen place within us that once was dead in sin before we came to Christ. In that late-night encounter with Nicodemus, Lord Jesus told the man seeking truth that he must be *born again* of the Spirit. The Lord was describing the spiritual CPR that takes place when a person receives Him as Lord (John 3:5-6). The point of our salvation when our once dead spirit is brought to life and filled with the Holy Spirit. This part of our being is where we commune with God, sense His presence and leading, and recognize that we are His children (Rev. 3:20, Romans 8:16).

We simply need to remember that our flesh – our selfishness and stuff that is the arena of our *soul* – profits nothing (John 6:63). When we come to the throne room no matter where we are – the laundry room, the boardroom, the coffee shop, or a sanctuary – the Holy Spirit within us is available to glorify Lord Jesus through us (John 16:14).

To worship in the spirit is to silence our thoughts that distract us, and humbly make a place for Him to take over. The Holy Spirit is awaiting our simple invitation to come and aid our worship. And come He will (Luke 11:13). Doing this may seem difficult at first, yet we must start somewhere even if our praise seems weak and tepid. Begin to praise in your known language and through the gift of spiritual language (tongues). Worship. Lift your praise. Adore. Repeat. Sense His presence and enter His gates of glory. This is worshiping in spirit as Lord Jesus invites us to do.

Invite Holy Spirit to worship through you. Write the phrases He gives you . . .

- _____
- _____
- _____
- _____
- _____
- _____
- _____
- _____
- _____
- _____

How does today's devotional speak to me personally?

_____

_____

_____

_____

_____

You are worthy, O Lord,
To receive glory and honor and power;
For You created all things, And by Your will they exist and were created.
Revelation 4:11

Write one phrase from this verse, ponder it, let your own worship begin . . .

_____

_____

_____

Day 9

With my lips I have declared All the judgments of Your mouth.
Psalm 119:13

The entirety of Your word is truth,
And every one of Your righteous judgments endures forever.
Psalm 119:160

What does it mean to worship in *truth* as Jesus instructed the woman at the well? Let's continue from yesterday . . .

There are certainly times we come to the gates of glory without a clue about where to begin our worship of Abba Father. Maybe our schedules have been, well, over-scheduled, or the strife of life has caught up to us. We are grateful for many things, but words of worship elude our minds. In times like these, to open God's Word and worship with believers through the ages can expand our spirit up to express the glory He is due.

God's Word is truth. We can never go wrong by turning to the Psalms and declaring the truth of Who our God is by reading His written word. Often, I will turn to Isaiah 6 or Ezekiel 1 and 2 to read the accounts of worship for these two prophets. And I love to join with John in Revelation 1-5, to peek in on and seize his worship experience for my own.

Worshiping in truth is not only the power of speaking and declaring praise that aligns with His Word; it also means worshipping through the truth that we are currently experiencing. Sometimes, that truth is painful, tragic, and tear-filled. We worship from the deep places of our being, knowing that Lord Jesus will be faithful in our dire situations. He will never give up on us. He has not forgotten us. He holds us close. He is victorious. When we worship amid what is true for us at the moment, the good, bad, or ugly, we touch the heart of the One who holds our every tear so tenderly.

This is powerful worship. This is worshiping in truth.

Ten worship statements that are true to me currently . . .

- _____
- _____
- _____
- _____
- _____
- _____
- _____
- _____
- _____
- _____

How does today's devotional speak to me personally?

_____
_____
_____
_____
_____

For we are the circumcision, who worship God in the Spirit,
rejoice in Christ Jesus, and have no confidence in the flesh,
Philippians 3:3

My prayer of invitation for the Holy Spirit's help . . .

_____
_____
_____
_____

Day 10

Serve the LORD with gladness;
Come before His presence with singing.
Know that the LORD, He is God;
It is He who has made us, and not we ourselves;
We are His people and the sheep of His pasture.
Psalm 100:2-3

Along with worshiping our magnificent Creator in spirit and truth, we need to remember two more things.

One, we are His lambs
Two, He is our Shepherd.

Pretty simple. Nevertheless, the waters can be oh so muddied sometimes.

There is a movement in our midst to declare we are capable, deserving, worthy, and can do it – whatever *it* is. Still, our human abilities are only just that – human (2 Corinthians 4:7). Anything eternal, anything of worth, or anything of goodness emanating from our lives will only be derived when we hide ourselves in Christ (Colossians 3:3). John the Baptist spoke the truth: *more of Him and less of me* (John 3:30).

Yes. I must remember these things. That I am His lamb – His most beloved lamb, even in my faults and failings, sinfulness and stuff. He alone brings worth to my life. Isn't this the truth? That when I live as His lamb relying implicitly upon Him as my Shepherd, Healer, Provider, Defender, and Father, sweet thankfulness rises from my life spontaneously. And not the other way around.

So, I ask as we head into worship today, what aspect of our lives are we trying to accomplish in our own strength? Kind of wearying, isn't it? As we exalt Him throughout our daily tasks, let's also lift this heavy load to Him of trying to perform and produce to prove our worth. Because truly, He alone is worthy, and we, ever and only, will find our worth in Him.

I am thankful to Him for these things today . . .

- _____
- _____
- _____
- _____
- _____
- _____
- _____
- _____
- _____
- _____

How does today's devotional speak to me personally?

_____
_____
_____
_____
_____

But we have this treasure in earthen vessels,
that the excellence of the power may be of God and not of us.
2 Corinthians 4:7

What does the verse above speak to my life?

_____
_____
_____
_____

Day 11

And you shall love the LORD your God with all your heart,
with all your soul, with all your mind, and with all your strength.
This is the first commandment.
Mark 12:30

Lord Jesus reminds us here of Moses' words in Deuteronomy 6:5. We find in the entirety of the Bible that He wants all of us, all the time, and this affects our thanks and praise. Loving God with every fiber of our being is another form of surrender – a tender hand-over to all that we hold dear.

The New Testament Word for *soul – psyche –* is that part of our life that includes our heart and emotions, mind and thoughts, intellect, the ability to choose, and our personality. These deep and ponderous wells of who we are is where the lifelong process of His redemption and sanctification takes place. Jesus wants to set free and restore the entirety of our soul. Possibly He speaks of these areas distinctly in the verse above because our hearts and minds – each part of our soul – need our continual attention and intentionality in loving and worshiping Him.

And then, Jesus speaks of our strength – our physical being – to love and worship Him thoroughly. The Bible invites us to exhibit our thanksgiving and devotion through lifted hands, dancing, kneeling, clapping, and lying prostrate. In the coming days, we will touch on these aspects of praise as we engage our hearts, minds, souls, and yes, our bodies to give Him the glory He is oh so worthy of.

Did you notice that Jesus doesn't mention our spirit in the verse above? Remember? Our spirit is that hidden portion of us where God dwells in the Person of the Holy Spirit. Before coming to Christ, our spirits were dead because of the terminal condition handed to us from the Garden (Ephesians 2:1). However, upon receiving Jesus (John 1:12), our spirits have been born again. This Holy Spirit filled place in us doesn't need to be reminded to worship like the rest of us does! Instead, let's be intentional to engage all the other aspects of our being – to love and adore Him.

Ten things I thank Him for with all my heart and mind...

- _____
- _____
- _____
- _____
- _____
- _____
- _____
- _____
- _____
- _____

How does today's devotional speak to me personally?

_____
_____
_____
_____

I beseech you therefore, brethren...
that you present your bodies a living sacrifice, holy, acceptable to God,
which is your reasonable service.
Romans 12:1

What does it mean for me to worship Him with my whole being?

_____
_____
_____
_____

Day 12

It is good to give thanks to the LORD,
And to sing praises to Your name, O Most High;
To declare Your lovingkindness in the morning,
And Your faithfulness every night,
Psalm 92:1-2

Okay. Here is the recipe for living positioned in the presence of the Lord all through our day. Every day.

What would it look like if our very first words to Jesus every morning were filled with thanksgiving, gratefulness, and worship? What if we started our days dancing into His courts with praise instead of lugging a laundry list of requests and needs? Even when life has its darkest tragedies and trials, what might our lives be like if we worshipped at His footstool because His compassion never fails and His mercies are new every morning? Might there be a chance that those verbal declarations to Him align our hearts and minds to expect a miracle for our trying situation? Just sayin'.

What about the end of our day? Could our sleep possibly be sweeter, longer, and deeper if each evening we declared His greatness over our lives? Thanking Him for His intimate knowledge of every detail that concerns us and speaking words of love to Him for how amazing He is? Often, the adversary of our souls uses the night watch to bring tormenting thoughts to our minds when we are facing health, financial, or relational issues. Nevertheless, might his tormenting voice be silenced if we pressed through to touch the hem of Jesus' garment as we worship Him before laying our heads on our pillows? I bet we would sleep more untroubled and unconcerned, hearing our own voice declare His greatness.

Again. We don't worship to get. However, when we speak praise, heaven touches earth, faith is released, and our Papa positions us for His plans and purposes. Beginning and ending our day and every moment in between, may His praise ever be on our lips. This sounds like a winning recipe indeed.

Morning or evening, here are ten things I love about the Lord . . .

- _____
- _____
- _____
- _____
- _____
- _____
- _____
- _____
- _____
- _____

How does today's devotional speak to me personally?

_____
_____
_____
_____

But each day the LORD pours his unfailing love upon me,
and through each night I sing his songs,
praying to God who gives me life.
Psalm 42:8 NLT

Ponder the verse above, then rewrite it in your own words. . .

_____
_____
_____
_____

Day 13

Oh, sing to the LORD a new song!
Sing to the LORD, all the earth.
Psalm 96:1

As a parent, I loved it when our children were small and made up their own songs. What delight! What joy! Every offkey melody, word, or phrase that didn't always make sense or rhyme brought sheer pleasure to my heart.

How does this apply to our study of worship?

Have you ever received a lovely store-bought card where the sender has only signed their name but not included a message of endearment? On the other hand, have you ever received a hand-made card, designed especially for you, with every detail bringing pleasure to your soul? The intentional thoughtfulness of the personally written note most likely meant more than the gift itself! Which of these two cards would you prefer to receive?

We can genuinely sing another person's worship song from our hearts. The Holy Spirit uses master musicians to woo us into the Lord's presence with beautiful lyrics and melodies that many of us could not come up with on our own. Surely God does give His body – the church – anointed worship leaders, musicians, writers, and artists. Nevertheless, the Psalmist invites us to step out of our comfort zones and make a new melody with our own words of adoration to the Lord (Psalm 40:3). Yikes! But oh, the reward of blessing our Father – even with our fumbling attempts!

Give it a try. Today. This moment.

Quietly at your workplace, marketplace, home, or school, begin a new song either in the Spirit or your known language to Jesus. Don't be concerned if the words are few and not perfectly phrased. Don't be discouraged if you don't know how to create a melody that anyone else might want to hear. You are singing to your Abba-Daddy and He is thrilled! Sense His delight and revel in His joy as hears your voice (Zephaniah. 3:17).

Ten things I am thankful for in this moment . . .

- _____
- _____
- _____
- _____
- _____
- _____
- _____
- _____
- _____
- _____

How does today's devotional speak to me personally?

_____
_____
_____
_____
_____

...Oh, sing to the LORD a new song!
For He has done marvelous things; His right hand and His holy arm have
gained Him the victory.
Psalm 98:1

My new song about something marvelous He has done for me . . .

_____
_____
_____

Day 14

Because Your lovingkindness is better than life,
My lips shall praise You.
Thus I will bless You while I live;
I will lift up my hands in Your name.
Psalm 63:3-4

Throughout the Scriptures, we find various physical postures in thanksgiving, praise, and worship that can tamper with our comfort. No matter your denominational background, we have either seen or heard of worship practices we may question. Nevertheless, we cannot deny that God's Word doesn't just invite us to worship our beloved King with words and songs of praise; it summons us to incorporate physical worship. Let's look at the blessed gift of lifting our hands.

Universally, the sign of surrender is the raising of our hands and arms above our heads. Yes, surrender is at the apex of every worship time. With hands lifted high, we are at our most vulnerable; we are not covering ourselves. We are not trying to preserve or protect ourselves. When I intentionally raise my hands (because like anything we do, even this gesture can become rote and meaningless), I am signifying my abandonment to God's rule and reign in my life.

When I place my hands out before me at waist level, it's as if I am bringing an offering. I am making an exchange of my stuff for His splendor. And as I extend my arms and hands intentionally to my side, it's as if I am saying, *have at me, Lord.*

And finally, perhaps the most endearing and sweet aspect of raising my hands to Abba, I am coming as a little child to my Wonder-full Father and exclaiming, *Daddy, You are the best! Please hold me!*

If you haven't yet practiced this form of worship, be encouraged to in the privacy of your time alone with Jesus or in your church setting. Both you and He will find great pleasure when you do.

Ten things I am grateful for in this moment . . .

- _____
- _____
- _____
- _____
- _____
- _____
- _____
- _____
- _____
- _____

How does today's devotional speak to me personally?

_____

_____

_____

_____

_____

Let my prayer be set before You as incense,
The lifting up of my hands as the evening sacrifice.
Psalm 141:2

Why might the lifting of my hands bless the Lord's heart?

_____

_____

_____

_____

Day 15

"You will not need to fight in this battle...
stand still and see the salvation of the LORD,
who is with you"...
And Jehoshaphat bowed his head ...worshiping the LORD.
...he appointed those who should sing to the LORD,
and who should praise the beauty of holiness,
as they went out before the army and were saying:
"Praise the LORD, For His mercy endures forever."
2 Chronicles 20:17-18, 20-21

This is one of my most favorite accounts from the Bible:

Israel is about to be creamed by the onslaught of enemy attack. King Jehoshaphat leads the nation to seek the Lord, and God speaks, giving them out-of-the-box instructions. Nevertheless, He promises complete victory. The nation responds and humbles itself, calls the worship team to the front of the line, and heads out to meet the assaulting army.

Pure and simple, the enemy is absolutely defeated. Better than defeated. The enemy turns inward and annihilates itself.

We discussed worship as warfare on Day 3, but we must remind ourselves of this truth. Worship is our battle cry. Worship is the standard we raise to face our adversaries (Isaiah 59:19). When we worship the Name above all names and genuinely let Holy Spirit adoration arise from our being, hell is stopped in its tracks. Really. Truly.

Do you have a burden, concern, question, or heartache? I encourage you to read the whole of 2 Chronicles 20. Seek the Lord (v. 3). Listen for the Lord's battle directions for your personal situation (v.15). Position yourself (v.17). Humble yourself (v.18). Choose to believe God (v. 20). Lift up verbal praise (v.21).

Repeat until victory is secured.

Write ten declarative statements about the Lord . . .

- _____
- _____
- _____
- _____
- _____
- _____
- _____
- _____
- _____
- _____

How does today's devotional speak to me personally?

_____

_____

_____

_____

Have I not commanded you?
Be strong and of good courage; do not be afraid,
Nor be dismayed, for the Lord your God is with you wherever you go.
Joshua 1:9

How does the verse above encourage my faith?

_____

_____

_____

_____

Day 16

Be anxious for nothing, but in everything by prayer
...with thanksgiving, let your requests be made known to God;
and the peace of God, which surpasses all understanding,
will guard your hearts and minds through Christ Jesus.
Philippians 4:6-7

I subscribe to a bunch of home-type magazines. When the Thanksgiving season rolls around the corner, turkey and sweet potato recipes abound, plus articles on cultivating gratefulness in our lives. Yes, indeed.

Scientific research reports that those with grateful, thankful hearts have less disease, less worry, less stress, less of just about every negative in the human condition. Honest. Just Google the subject. *Science is learning what God's Word has said all along* as Christian neuroscientist Dr. Caroline Leaf often states.[2]

Thankfulness is key.

In the passage above, Paul isn't telling us to be thankful *for* the stuff in our lives that are currently testing us – but to be grateful the Lord Jesus is BIGGER than all our stuff. When anxiety wants to rule our hearts and minds, the direct antidote is gratefulness and thanksgiving as we earnestly lay our every care and concern at His feet and *leave it there*. Yes, leave it there with Him and don't get up until you sense His peace. As a by-product, this is how we better learn to hear Jesus' voice with clarity and cultivate His felt presence in our lives.

The world on its own doesn't really know *Who* to be grateful to. Honestly, it is kind of funny when I read these magazine articles about gratefulness. However, *we* know where every source of goodness and light in our lives comes from (James 1:17). Keeping at the forefront of our minds, the incredible works He has done in our lives, and all He has given us allow His peace to reign in our souls. Gratefulness recounts that He moved our mountains many times in the past, and *He will* do it again. Yes, He will.

Ten things am I grateful for . . .

- _____
- _____
- _____
- _____
- _____
- _____
- _____
- _____
- _____
- _____

How does today's devotional speak to me personally?

_____

_____

_____

_____

Oh, magnify the Lord with me. And let us exalt His name together.
I sought the Lord, and He heard me,
And delivered me from all my fears.
Psalm 34:3-4

What phrase from the verse above speaks to my heart and why?

_____

_____

_____

_____

Day 17

Then He said, "Take now your son, your only son Isaac, whom you love
. . . and offer him there as a burnt offering . . ."
And Abraham said to his young men, "Stay here with the donkey;
the lad and I will go yonder and worship,
and we will come back to you."
Genesis 22:2, 5

We opened our *Thirty Days of Thanksgiving* with surrender. Now, let's look at a specific type of surrender as worship.

When we lay down our dreams, our precious God-given gifts, and even include His future personal promises to us as a sacrifice of praise, we arrive at a place in our hearts of truly trusting the Lord and bringing Him glory. Doing this, cuts to the core of our being. When we release into our Good Shepherd's hand, all that we hold dear to our hearts now, and all our hopes for what is to come.

Abraham tells his servants that he is going to worship, yet he fully understands what is about to happen. God is requiring the surrender of Abraham's beloved son, the much-promised heir upon whom hinges other far-reaching future promises that will affect the nations of the world.

Ponder what this means for your life at this moment. I mean seriously. Do this. What do you hold dearest? What prospective dreams and hopes for the future give you a reason to wake up each morning? If we are honest, surrendering them to the Lord takes our breath away when we think of these things.

And yet, Abraham's true worship is that He knows God's love, mercy, and grace are greater, bigger, and perfect. Abe doesn't know how, but he tells the servants that both he and Isaac *will return*. He declares in v.8 that Father *will* provide. He will do something *even more* breathtaking. This is true worship: fully trusting the Lord and *His* outcome. Let's worship Him.

I am surrendering these near and dear things to Jesus' care . . .

- _____
- _____
- _____
- _____
- _____
- _____
- _____
- _____
- _____
- _____

How does today's devotional speak to me personally?

_____

_____

_____

_____

I will worship toward Your holy temple,
And praise Your name for Your lovingkindness and Your truth;
. . . The Lord will perfect that which concerns me;
Your mercy, O Lord, endures forever;
Psalm 138:2, 8

What does it mean for me to know God will perfect those things I care about?

_____

_____

_____

Day 18

. . . the twenty-four elders fell down before the Lamb,
each having a harp,
and golden bowls full of incense, which are the prayers of the saints.
And they sang a new song, saying:
"You are worthy. . .
Revelation 5:8-9

In John's grand revelation, he is escorted into the heavenly realms of God's throne room (Revelation 4). The angelic hosts are worshiping Lord Jesus, the Lamb of God. The elders around the throne are holding harps as worship instruments. They are also holding golden bowls containing the prayers of the saints. These are *our* prayers.

As the curtain is pulled back to reveal this scene, we glimpse a powerful aspect of worship and prayer that takes place when both prayer and worship are combined. This manner of intercession and praise has taken on the name *Harp and Bowl Ministry*.

When we bless the Lord with our genuine, truth-full, and Spirit-led thanksgiving, praise, and worship, we are the recipients of realizing the greatness of our God in the light of our lives. When our adoration peels back the curtain and we enter the Holy of Holies, our prayers become powerful. The incense of our intercession transforms from the urgency of our need for the greatness of our God. Then, worshipful prayer stands on the platform of who God is, not from our fears that He is not enough.

Harp and bowl worship/intercession is very practical. When sustained prayer is called for, adding to our worship, especially when music is employed, is often easier to maintain than when we only pray. And the impact is immeasurable. Ann Voskamp writes, *prayer without ceasing is only possible in a life of continual thanks. How did I ever think there was another way to enter into His courts but with thanksgiving?*[3]

Let's pray . . . and worship.

Five prayer requests and five phrases of praise . . .

- _____
- _____
- _____
- _____
- _____
- _____
- _____
- _____
- _____
- _____

How does today's devotional speak to me personally?

_____
_____
_____
_____

Every morning you'll hear me at it again.
Every morning I lay out the pieces of my life on your altar
and watch for fire to descend.
Psalm 5:3

How might mingling my prayers with worship be helpful to me?

_____
_____
_____
_____

Day 19

Then David danced before the LORD with all his might;
and David was wearing a linen ephod.
2 Samuel 6:14

Although there are many accounts of King David's romance with God found in the Old Testament, surely this story of David's dancing before the Lord with all his might in worship surpasses every one of them.

David doesn't care what people think – including his wife. He doesn't care how undignified he might seem or how off-the-charts-nutso he might appear. David is worshiping with abandon the Almighty as the Ark of the Covenant returns to Jerusalem. The very presence of God – under the Old Testament – is returning to His people. If anything can cause an explosion of unbridled praise, God's presence is first and foremost.

David's display of untamed joy, effervescent emotion, and unadulterated adoration comes from a deep well within him of the Father's nearness, care, and power. David is not just a king; he is El Shaddai's friend. David *knows* the Lord.

Yet, for us, of all the physical elements of worship, dancing probably receives the least amount of attention. It can make us feel clumsy and uncomfortable. It can be misunderstood or rendered inappropriate. Yet, we cannot deny the power and beauty of dancing in worship as seen in the Scriptures. Dance is the celebration of God's might and His miracles.

In the embrace of the New Covenant we live in – God's presence no longer is manifest in the Ark. His presence now lives *in us* by the power of the Holy Spirit (Colossians 1:27, John 7:39).

God lives in us. Let's take a moment and ponder this wonder. I mean really. Let's stop and allow this truth to drip into our hearts and minds. And next? Let's dance with David before Him.

Ten things I could dance before Jesus about...

- _____
- _____
- _____
- _____
- _____
- _____
- _____
- _____
- _____
- _____

How does today's devotional speak to me personally?

_____
_____
_____
_____

Praise Him with the timbrel and dance;
Praise Him with stringed instruments and flutes!
Psalm 150:4

What fills my heart as I think about celebrating God?

_____
_____
_____
_____

Day 20

But You are holy,
Enthroned in the praises of Israel.
Psalms 22:3

From the heart of this Messianic psalm, we learn one of the most important aspects of worship and thanksgiving. When we rightfully declare God's kingdom rule in every area of our lives, His kingdom power and presence are made known.

One of God's magnificent, beyond comprehension attributes is His omnipresence: the ability to be everywhere at once. He is always with us. He is always everywhere. No place of His creation is exempt from His presence, not even hell itself (Psalm 139:8).

And yet, we find throughout God's Word where men and women encountered His *manifest presence*. We know this in our personal experience as well. These are times when we encounter His reality through the presence of the Holy Spirit in our spirit. We *sense and feel* His presence in our emotions, thoughts, and physical being.

The Lord Jesus wants to reveal Himself to us through the power of the Holy Spirit within us (John 16:14). Psalm 22:3 teaches us that as we declare His Lordship, we create a place – a throne – for His felt and experienced presence and rule in our lives. As our praises enthrone Him – literally make a seat for Him – we experience His very felt presence far surpassing mere head knowledge. And wherever King Jesus is, just as we read in the Gospels, there is salvation, healing, and deliverance.

Does your home or workplace need to experience heaven's rule today? Could your body use His healing touch? Do you need some divine intervention or direction? Begin to praise. Declare His Lordship in the rooms of your home, work, body, or soul (your heart and mind) and watch what happens when Lord Jesus takes His rightful throne.

Thanksgiving

Ten worship statements for establishing His presence today . . .

- _____
- _____
- _____
- _____
- _____
- _____
- _____
- _____
- _____
- _____

How does today's devotional speak to me personally?

_____
_____
_____

And he said: "Lord God of Israel,
there is no God in heaven or on earth like You,"
. . . When Solomon had finished praying . . . the priests could not enter the
house of the Lord, because the glory of the Lord
had filled the Lord's house.
2 Chronicles 6:14, 7:1-2

What areas of my daily life need His presence and rule?

_____
_____
_____

Day 21

In this manner, therefore, pray:
Our Father in heaven, Hallowed be Your name.
Your kingdom come.
Your will be done on earth as it is in heaven.
Matthew 6:9-10

Today's lesson follows on the heels of yesterday's study: when we worship, heaven comes down.

This simple prayer outline that Lord Jesus gives - which we call *The Lord's Prayer* - is a doozy. And it starts with our declaring who God is. Our Father. Our Abba-Daddy who loves us beyond reason. When this truth becomes rock solid heart knowledge for us, our faith is pretty much invincible. Yes. *OUR* Father. Yours and mine. And His Name – no other name – is HOLY.

All prayer should begin with worship and thanks. When we get that right, our prayer requests pretty much take care of themselves. When our alone times begin with worshiping in spirit and truth, and we have created a place where we sense His felt presence, almost nothing else that concerns us matters. We know He has us *and* our burdens. When we lean into Daddy's embrace – and stay there – we begin to comprehend that He already understands what we need (Matthew 6:8). Help is on the way.

Because our praise brings heaven down, asking for His will to be accomplished is not passive acquiescence but spiritual warfare at its most potent and dynamic. We are declaring God's rule and reign usurping any and every plan of the enemy or flesh that is waging war against us. It is here we receive His invitation to partner with Him in battle prayer for our lives, our homes, our communities, and the nations (1 Corinthians 3:9).

And it all begins with our lifting Spirit-filled adoration as we climb into our Father's arms.

Ten praise declarations over my circumstances...

- _____
- _____
- _____
- _____
- _____
- _____
- _____
- _____
- _____
- _____

How does today's devotional speak to me personally?

_____

_____

_____

But when you pray, go into your room,
...(and) pray to your Father who is in the secret place; and your Father
who sees in secret will reward you openly...
For your Father knows the things you have need of before you ask Him.
Matthew 6:6, 8

How do the verses above encourage my heart and prayers?

_____

_____

_____

_____

_____

Day 22

Therefore by Him let us continually offer the sacrifice of praise to God,
that is, the fruit of our lips, giving thanks to His name.
Hebrews 13:15

We encountered Abraham's indescribable willingness to offer a worship sacrifice, however, what might a *sacrifice of praise* mean for us?

The Book of Hebrews was written to Jewish believers who endured tremendous tribulation and persecution because of their newfound faith in Christ (Hebrews 10:32-33). Could the call to offer a continual sacrifice of praise mean worshiping when they, along with us, feel like it is the last thing we would want to do?

When we are hurting, broken, or facing tragic circumstances, praising God is often the furthest thing from our minds. The enemy of our soul may be using our vulnerability in these situations to entice us to allow anger and unbelief to gain ground in our lives. The devil's strategy is *always* to distract us from the love of God and ultimately destroy us (John 10:10).

To walk in thanksgiving and praise during challenging times often begins as a sacrifice on our part. It requires something of us that we don't necessarily want to give. King David put it this way – *I will not offer worship that does not cost me* (2 Samuel 24:24). At first, sacrificial worship *will* require a cost from us. When our flesh is weak, it is easier to question and be upset with the Lord than to give Him praise when we don't understand what is going on. We may also be sacrificing, on His altar, our pride, and selfish self-will.

These trying times are when we need to worship ardently and boldly. Hell has touched us, and it needs to stop. When our lips speak Who we know Jesus is, it *is a sacrifice the enemy hears and fears.* And we, who are proclaiming the praise of the Commander of the Heavenly Hosts, will be strengthened by His Spirit as He decisively wins our battles for us.

Ten phrases of love to my Abba-Daddy ...

- _____
- _____
- _____
- _____
- _____
- _____
- _____
- _____
- _____
- _____

How does today's devotional speak to me personally?

_____

_____

_____

_____

. . . you also as living stones, are being built up a spiritual house,
a holy priesthood, to offer up spiritual sacrifices
acceptable to God through Jesus Christ
1 Peter 2:5

What does it mean for me to offer a sacrifice of praise?

_____

_____

_____

_____

Day 23

And He took bread, gave thanks and broke it, and gave it to them, saying,
"This is My body which is given for you;
do this in remembrance of Me."
Luke 22:19

Lord Jesus, on the night of His betrayal, worshiped the Father with holy thanks, knowing that his body would be broken, scourged, pierced, and nailed only a few short hours later. With even more heart-rending consequence, Jesus knew His Father would have to turn His face from Him who bore all our sin, sickness, wretchedness, and brokenness.

Jesus gave thanks as He instituted communion – His last supper with His disciples – until all believers will share supper again with Him at His marriage feast (Revelation 19:9). And Communion is often called the *Eucharist* – the beautiful Greek word meaning to give thanks or thanksgiving, with the Greek word *charis* or *grace* smack dab in the middle of it.

Author Ann Voskamp, from her book, *One Thousand Gifts*, writes:

> *Eucharisteo means "to give thanks," and give is a verb, something that we do. God calls me to do thanks. To give the thanks away. That thanks-giving might literally become thanks-living. That our lives become the very blessings we have received. I am blessed. I can bless. Imagine! I could let Him make me the gift! I could be the joy![4]*

Just as Jesus gave thanks as He broke the bread, when we give thanks to our Father, there is a breaking in us, too. In worship and gratefulness, we come to realize that we really are dust without Him. This would seem to cause us to question our worth, but instead, in our Father's great love, our thanksgiving elevates our position. We recognize how beloved and valued we genuinely are.

Ten things I am thankful for today...

- _____
- _____
- _____
- _____
- _____
- _____
- _____
- _____
- _____
- _____

How does today's devotional speak to me personally?

_____
_____
_____
_____

> *... O LORD, our Lord, How excellent is Your name in all the earth,*
> *... What is man that You are mindful of him,*
> *And the son of man that You visit him?*
> Psalm 8:1, 4

How does the verse above encourage my heart?

_____
_____
_____
_____

Day 24

Oh come, let us worship and bow down;
Let us kneel before the LORD our Maker.
Psalm 95:6

Sometimes when we come before the Lord, we just need a little faceplant in the carpet time. There is something about bowing, kneeling, or lying prostrate, as God's Word beckons us to do, which puts us in our place. And God in His in our thoughts and emotions.

We see throughout the Scriptures, from Genesis to Revelation, great men and women of faith who revered the Lord with the physical act of bowing, kneeling, or stretching full out before Him. There is something powerful for our enemy, the devil, to observe as we humble ourselves in thanksgiving and praise – our humility strikes a blow to his pride. And our pride, too.

When we bow our knees, or we lay prostrate, we are in a most vulnerable position. Even those younger and agile among us find that flight and escape are impeded from this position. Kneeling declares that we are surrendering (again!) and submitting to His authority. Our posture states we are not looking for Plans B, C, or D, but rather, we are trusting His supreme and love-consumed plan for what we face.

Come, let us worship and bow down, is first and foremost, an attitude of the heart (again!). We may be able to bow physically, yet what is our heart doing? Any act of worship can become rote and routine, losing its fervency and meaning. Forever and always, Jesus is after our hearts.

Whatever your custom of worship, it might be time to add this to your repertoire. If it isn't physically possible for you to kneel, simply bow what you can. Maybe that sounds silly but kneeling or lying prone isn't casual stuff. It takes intentional effort. And when the Spirit calls us to come humbly bow before Him, let's heed His call, and prostrate ourselves before the King of all Kings upon His throne.

Ten of His attributes I worship Him for today...

- _____
- _____
- _____
- _____
- _____
- _____
- _____
- _____
- _____
- _____

How does today's devotional speak to me personally?

_____
_____
_____
_____

Therefore God also has highly exalted Him
and given Him the name which is above every name,
that at the name of Jesus every knee should bow...
Philippians 2:9-10

What does the all-powerful name of Jesus mean to me?

_____
_____
_____
_____

Day 25

May you always be filled with the fruit of your salvation—
the righteous character produced in your life by Jesus Christ—
for this will bring much glory and praise to God.
Philippians 1:11 NLT

Honestly. How we live matters.

No, this isn't legalism or trying by our efforts to earn God's favor, but we do need to be thoughtful about what we say and do. Really. The world is watching. Watching to see if Jesus is the real deal like we know He is.

We are recognizing that thanksgiving, praise, and worship are a lifestyle. It is *thanks-living,* as we learned from Ann Voskamp a few days ago. Paul, several times in his letters to the various early churches, encouraged the believers to walk worthy of God's calling upon their lives (Ephesians 4:1, Colossians 1:1). Glorifying Him isn't only when we are with our church family or in our quiet times; it is *all* the time.

Spirit-inspired worship is what we have been learning, but how much more will Spirit-inspired living bring Him glory? A lot. A lot more (John 6:63). So, we might need a paradigm shift in how we do life. How about some Holy Spirit alterations? Asking Him to go deep within our hearts and free us from some old ways and habits that hinder our testimony for the Gospel. Remember the old anecdote, *Lord, so far, I haven't blown-it – but I am getting out of bed now, and I need Your help!*

Yes, we need His help. We can't fix ourselves, but Jesus can do the job plenty well. The verse above states*: our righteous character will be the work of Jesus Himself.* Do whatever it takes to get free in Him: see your pastor or find a Christian counselor. Make yourself accountable to those you trust to walk you through and out of whatever strongholds or hindrances that limit His life overflowing in you. And above all, keep falling more ardently in love with Him. Ultimately, we will look more and more like the One we cherish and adore and worship.

Areas in my life that could use some Holy Spirit tune-up...

- _____
- _____
- _____
- _____
- _____
- _____
- _____
- _____
- _____
- _____

How does today's devotional speak to me personally?

_____

_____

_____

_____

. . . that you may walk worthy of the Lord,
fully pleasing Him, being fruitful in every good work
and increasing in the knowledge of God;
Colossians 1:10

What does it mean for me to walk worthy of the Lord?

_____

_____

_____

_____

Day 26

But when the chief priests and scribes saw
the wonderful things that He did,
and the children crying out in the temple and saying,
"Hosanna to the Son of David!"
. . . and said to Him, "Do You hear what these are saying?"
And Jesus said to them, "Yes. Have you never read,
'Out of the mouth of babes and nursing infants
You have perfected praise'?"
Matthew 21:15-16

Children always get it right. You know. No filter, no sophistication, ultra-spontaneous, no presumption – simply speaking what they see and hear literally. What they know to be true.

As Jesus entered the temple, where the priests and Sanhedrin were lying in wait for His capture, all sorts of bedlam was taking place. In righteous anger, Jesus began overturning the temple tables, coins of currency were scattered, and fur from the sacrificial animals was flying. Everyone was in an uproar. And in the middle of it all, the children began to sing.

Yes, there is something about excellence in the church that has profound meaning. We *should* do our best and give our all to any endeavor for His Kingdom. Yesterday, I encouraged a young, anointed worship pastor to head back to school to perfect her ability to worship and better mentor those under her tutelage. Nevertheless, when our pursuit of perfect becomes more about the pursuit of performance, we have crossed a line somewhere.

So, let's never forget the way children worship Him. Oh, if we could just take their cue in praise and thanksgiving. Unfiltered, unsophisticated, spontaneous, and not always perfectly pitched, because it is our hearts, He longs for most.

Yes, out of the mouths of babes – we could learn a thing or two...

Ten things I am thankful for...

- _____
- _____
- _____
- _____
- _____
- _____
- _____
- _____
- _____
- _____

How does today's devotional speak to me personally?

_____
_____
_____
_____
_____

Therefore whoever humbles himself as this little child
is the greatest in the kingdom of heaven.
Matthew 18:4

What does becoming child-like (not childish) mean to me?

_____
_____
_____
_____

Day 27

For a day in Your courts is better than a thousand.
I would rather be a doorkeeper in the house of my God
Than dwell in the tents of wickedness.
Psalm 84:10

Nothing compares with the felt presence of the Living God. As King David speaks to us through the ages in Psalm 16:11, *in His presence is fullness and joy and at His right hand are pleasures forevermore.*

Anna knew about this place of incredible blessing. The few short verses found in Luke 2:36-38, tell us of a woman who experienced much tragedy and sadness when she lost the husband of her youth. However, we discover that Anna found even greater treasure and fulfillment to replace her loss in the presence of the Lord in the temple. God's Word so simply but profoundly tells us, *she served God with fasting and prayers night and day.*

Anna positioned herself as a doorkeeper in the house of God.

Now, back to us. How do we feel or sense God's presence? This is the work of the Holy Spirit (Romans 8:16), the third person of the Godhead. He is coequal, co-divine, co-existent, and co-eternal with the Father and the Son and He dwells within each of us who have received Jesus by faith (John 1:12). Jesus told us the Holy Spirit would manifest the presence of the Lord to us (John 16:14). How does He do that? Yes, most certainly, the veracity of God's Word tells us this. But it is also, the confirmation experienced deep within our spirit that we belong irrevocably to the Father (Romans 8:16) and that we are now His temple (1 Corinthians 3:16).

So, to be a doorkeeper in the King's court. Easily offering praise and adoration from our overflowing sense of His presence throughout the day, every day. No matter where we are or how hectic life can get. This is the high calling and privilege of every believer. This is life in excess. Nothing compares. Nothing fulfills. Nothing satisfies, like the very presence of God. Let's be doorkeepers too.

Ten wonder-full things Jesus has done in my life...

- _____
- _____
- _____
- _____
- _____
- _____
- _____
- _____
- _____
- _____

How does today's devotional speak to me personally?

_____

_____

_____

_____

Come, let's shout praises to God,
raise the roof for the Rock who saved us!
Let's march into his presence singing praises,
lifting the rafters with our hymns!
Psalm 95:1 MSG

How am I encouraged or challenged by these verses?

_____

_____

_____

Day 28

They sing the song of Moses, the servant of God,
and the song of the Lamb, saying:
"Great and marvelous are Your works,
Lord God Almighty! Just and true are Your ways,
O King of the saints!"
Revelation 15:3

Amid John's grand, unparalleled revelation of the end times, the Holy Spirit reveals to him those saints who have been victorious over the evil, end-time, beast. These believers who did not succumb to the beast or his wicked ways are now in heaven singing worship and thanks to the Most High after enduring probably the most horrific circumstances the world will have ever known or seen. They sing the song of Moses...

The song of Moses, found in Exodus 15, takes place after the miraculous crossing of the Red Sea. The Israelites are rejoicing. They are over-the-top jubilant. They are dancing, they are speaking – most likely shouting – and singing. They are ever so grateful and thankful.

We need to take a cue from these folks. Great deliverance beckons even greater and audacious praise. We not only need to find release from the weight of having walked through the dark times in our lives but appropriately offer crazy worship to the One who brought us through (Isaiah 43:1-3).

When the lame man in Acts 3:1-10 received the miracle of strength in his legs upon Peter declaring healing to him in the name of Jesus, he began walking and leaping and praising God. I am pretty sure he wasn't doing this quietly.

What has the Lord done for you? What darkness has He plucked you from to bring you into His marvelous light? Recall circumstance after difficult circumstance. And then offer some out-of-your-comfort-zone adoration to Him.

Ten things I am grateful for...

- _____
- _____
- _____
- _____
- _____
- _____
- _____
- _____
- _____
- _____

How does today's devotional speak to me personally?

_____

_____

_____

*That you may really come to know – practically, through experience for
yourselves – the love of Christ, which far surpasses mere knowledge
without experience; that you may be filled...unto all the fullness of God
...and become a body wholly filled and flooded with God Himself!*
Ephesians 3:18-19 AMPC (Brackets removed)

How does the verse above touch my heart?

_____

_____

_____

_____

Day 29

As you therefore have received Christ Jesus the Lord,
so walk in Him, rooted and built up in Him
and established in the faith, as you have been taught,
abounding in it with thanksgiving.
Colossians 2:6-7

The apostle Paul writes frequently about faith being rooted and established in the infinite love of God (Ephesians 3:14-21). Mind you, Paul is not talking about some flimsy root system where a tree bowls over whenever a storm or tempest blows but a root system that goes deep with both intellectual knowledge *and* first-hand experience of God's love in the power and presence of the Holy Spirit. These roots enable the tree to stand firm no matter how violent, harsh, or unrelenting the winds of adversity are (Jeremiah 17:8). This type of faith has as its marker – abounding praise.

No, not flimsy, shallow thanksgiving, but effusive, extra-ordinary, over-the-top, excessive, overflowing worship. Gulp.

Do I live in that kind of faith choosing to trust Him over fear or worry; choosing to believe His Word over the enemy's whispers? Do I eagerly surrender all my concerns into His more than capable hands?

The Scriptures speak of a sweet, never-ending cycle. Trusting Jesus brings peace and joy. Peace and joy bubble over into thanksgiving and praise. Offering thanksgiving and praise for all He has done encourages my faith. My faith releases heaven's bounty and the demise of the enemy's work in my life. And if what I am going through currently still seems dim, the Holy Spirit will take me to the next level of trust, rejoicing, and faith by resting in the certainty that His grace *is* more than sufficient and He *is* at work (2 Corinthians 12:9).

Today, let's meditate upon and revel in God's beyond reason love, surrendering our every care, and letting our thanksgiving abound.

Ten things I will trust the Lord for...

- _____
- _____
- _____
- _____
- _____
- _____
- _____
- _____
- _____
- _____

How does today's devotional speak to me personally?

_____
_____
_____

O God, You are my God; Early will I seek You;
My soul thirsts for You . . . In a dry and thirsty land . . .
So I have looked for You in the sanctuary,
To see Your power and Your glory
Psalm 63:1-2

I will rewrite this verse in my own words.

_____
_____
_____
_____

Day 30

Be still, and know that I am God;
I will be exalted among the nations,
I will be exalted in the earth!
Psalm 46:10

Here, we find that our silence is worship too.

When we are done lifting our praise and gratitude, silence has its place before His throne. He summons us in this verse to come and be like Mary, who sat at His feet (Luke 10:39). When we silence our voice, and all we can discern is the sound of our breathing, we realize that God truly does hold our breath in His hand, and nothing in this life matters except Him (Daniel 5:23). And from this knowledge, He graciously aligns us to His Kingdom purposes. We remember that we were made for more. More than merely eking out a living until we draw our final breath. Our silence stills our being in the presence of Eternity.

There are promises in the verse above. First, this incredible understanding that our silence brings us into a greater depth of knowing the Lord Almighty. After thirty-seven chapters of Job and his four friends arguing, complaining, and correcting each other, when the talk was stilled – God spoke. The outcome? Job's humble cry, *"I have heard of You by the hearing of the ear, but now my eye sees You."* (Job 42:3, 5).

The second promise? When we participate in quiet adoration, leaning into His presence, a powerful dynamic in the spiritual realm occurs. He is exalted among the nations; He is exalted in the earth! As Dick Eastman writes, *"Here we discover that being silent in God's presence, as an act of worship, is linked to impacting the nations."*[5]

The close to our devotional is our continuing worship of the One Who loves us beyond comprehension, and is worthy of all our praise, all the time. Let's come and delight His heart with our lives *and* our worship.

Ten attributes of Lord Jesus I worship Him for...

- _____
- _____
- _____
- _____
- _____
- _____
- _____
- _____
- _____
- _____

How does today's devotional speak to me personally?

_____
_____
_____
_____
_____

Silence is praise to you, Zion-dwelling God,
And also obedience. You hear the prayer in it all.
Psalm 65:1 MSG

How do I think being silent in worship will impact my walk with God?

_____
_____
_____
_____

[1] Randy Remington, President: International Church of the Foursquare Gospel, *Converge Event*, Santa Clarita, CA - September 23-24, 2019

[2] Caroline Leaf, *Switch On Your Brain* (Baker Books, Grand Rapids, Michigan, 2013) p.13

[3] Ann Voskamp, One Thousand Gifts (Zondervan, Grand Rapids, Michigan, 2010) p.60

[4] Ann Voskamp, *One Thousand Gifts* (Zondervan, Grand Rapids, Michigan, 2010)

[5] Dick Eastman, *Intercessory Worship* (Chosen Books, Bloomington, Minnesota, 2011) p.37

Sue Boldt and her husband, Randy, have been senior pastors in northern California for over forty years. They minister and teach for Youth With a Mission (YWAM) in Taipei, Taiwan. Currently living in Los Angeles, they have a marriage retreat ministry, *A Regal Romance*, and they mentor and counsel younger pastors/ministry leaders at home and abroad. As a retreat and event speaker, Sue also facilitates a healing for life's hurts ministry, *Steps to Breakthrough* and she is currently engaged in forming a new women's conference, *Equip*. She has authored several self-published books and Bible studies: *Refresh, Pneuma Life, Morning Moments*, and a discipleship series for men and women entitled *CrossPointe*.

Subscribe to Sue's website www.sueboldt.com for weekly devotionals, Morning Moments of Prayer, upcoming sharing events, Bible studies (short videos that you can use to do CrossPointe with her!), books, and to contact her with questions or speaking engagement inquiries. She would love to hear from you!

Sue is also active on social media:

Facebook:
    Sue Boldt Crosspointe
    Crosspointe Online Bible Study

Instagram:
    @sueboldt_crosspointe
    @crosspointe_biblestudy

YouTube:
    Sue Boldt

All of Sue's Bible studies may be purchased on her website and www.amazon.com.

Made in United States
North Haven, CT
26 October 2022

25972926R00039